BULLDOGS

By Tammy Gagne

Consultant: Sharon Dykes, Chairperson
Bulldog Club of America Education Committee

Capstone
press

Mankato, Minnesota

Edge Books are published by Capstone Press,
151 Good Counsel Drive, P.O. Box 669, Mankato, Minnesota 56002.
www.capstonepress.com

022010
005705R

Library of Congress Cataloging-in-Publication Data
Gagne, Tammy.
    Bulldogs / by Tammy Gagne.
    p. cm. — (Edge books. All about dogs.)
    Includes bibliographical references and index.
    ISBN-13: 978-1-4296-1952-3 (hardcover)
    ISBN-10: 1-4296-1952-X (hardcover)
    1. Bulldog — Juvenile literature. I. Title. II. Series.
SF429.B85G347 2009
636.72 — dc22   2008001220

Summary: Describes the history, physical features, temperament, and care of
    the bulldog breed.

Editorial Credits
Erika L. Shores, editor; Veronica Bianchini, designer; Marcie Spence,
    photo researcher

Photo Credits
BigStockPhoto.com/Tammy McAllister, 19
Capstone Press/Karon Dubke, cover, 1, 5, 6, 9 (bottom), 10, 15 (bottom), 16, 17,
    18, 22, 25, 26, 27, 28
Cheryl A. Ertelt, 24
CH Seabright Silver Saber Bred by Seabright Bulldogs; owned and loved by
    Calvin and Sharon Dykes, Bigfoot Bulldogs, 15 (top)
Corbis/LWA-Dann Tardif, 29
iStockphoto/Heiko Potthoff, 21; Shaun Lowe, 12
Jim Lopes/123RF, 11
Mary Evans Picture Library, 9 (top)

**Capstone Press thanks Martha Diedrich, dog trainer, for her assistance
    with this book.**

Table of Contents

A Funny Frown 4

History of Bulldogs 8

Wrinkles and Short Legs 14

Caring for a Bulldog 20

Glossary 30

Read More 31

Internet Sites 31

Index 32

CHAPTER 1

A FUNNY FROWN

It's not surprising that the bulldog is the official mascot of the United States Marines. This rugged dog breed shares many qualities with this branch of the armed forces. Like Marines, bulldogs are strong, bold, and loyal.

The funny frown of a bulldog can bring a smile to anyone's face. These friendly dogs make wonderful pets for the right people.

The Dog For You?

The American Kennel Club (AKC) divides dog breeds into seven groups. They are the herding, hound, sporting, terrier, toy, working, and non-sporting groups. Bulldogs belong to the non-sporting group. This group includes breeds that do not fit into any of the other six AKC groups.

The non-sporting group title fits the bulldog. Very active people make poor owners for this breed. A bulldog will gladly go for a walk. But a long hike or run might be too much for this short-legged pooch.

A wrinkly, frowning face makes it easy to identify a bulldog.

Responsible breeders produce healthy bulldog puppies.

EDGE FACT

Most bulldogs can't swim. Some owners put a life jacket on their bulldog to keep the dog afloat in water.

Finding a Bulldog

Once you decide that you want to add a bulldog to your family, the next step is finding the right dog. The best way to find a bulldog puppy is through a **breeder.** The Bulldog Club of America lists breeders throughout the United States. The club can help you find a good breeder in your area.

The cost of a bulldog puppy is quite high. The price reflects that most bulldogs are delivered by cesarean section. The mother goes through surgery in order for her pups to be born.

Adoption is another great way to find a bulldog. Many bulldogs at animal shelters or breed rescue groups make fine pets. These organizations help match interested families with bulldogs in need of new homes.

breeder — someone who breeds
and raises dogs or other animals

CHAPTER 2

HISTORY OF BULLDOGS

The word "bulldog" was first used in the late 1700s. Bullbaiting was very popular in England at this time. People would gather at bullbaiting events to watch dogs fight bulls. The dogs used in these contests were bred to be fearless and strong.

The object was for the dog to pin a bull to the ground by biting its nose. This event was very painful for the bull and dangerous for the dog. Many bulldogs were stabbed or thrown into the air by the bulls' horns. Many dogs died, but this fact mattered little to the bloodthirsty fans.

Fortunately, not everyone approved of these contests. Many people thought the sport was cruel. Bullbaiting was eventually outlawed in 1835. Still, the bulldog's name remained. It will forever be a reminder of the breed's past.

Hundreds of years ago, bulldogs were trained to attack bulls and pin them to the ground.

Saving the Breed

After bullbaiting was outlawed, a new problem developed. Demand for bulldogs quickly dropped. A group of English bulldog fans saved the breed from disappearing. They formed the first bulldog club in 1864. This early organization only lasted three years, but its members created the first bulldog standard. This **breed standard** describes the ideal features of a particular breed.

A second and longer-lasting bulldog club formed in London, England, in 1875. The Bulldog Club of America formed in 1890. This was the same year the AKC accepted the bulldog as an official breed.

breed standard — the physical features of a breed that judges look for in a dog show

The French bulldog
is smaller than its
bulldog cousin.

What Kind of Bulldog
Is That?

Today, the bulldog is a popular pet throughout the world.
Some people refer to this breed as the English bulldog. In
the United States, the official name for the breed does not
include the word English. The breed is simply called the
bulldog. The French bulldog, however, is a separate breed.

Bull mastiffs, like the one shown here, have longer legs than bulldogs.

You may have heard the term "bull breeds." These breeds include the bull terrier and the bull mastiff. The bulldog was **crossbred** with the terrier and mastiff breeds, as well as the French bulldog, to develop these breeds.

Today, bulldogs are smaller and gentler than the bulldogs used in bullbaiting. Early bulldogs weighed as much as 100 pounds (45 kilograms). Modern bulldogs are about half this size. Dogs used in bullbaiting were also raised to be extremely aggressive. Today, one couldn't ask for a kinder pet than the bulldog. Its body may be smaller, but its heart is truly big.

EDGE FACT

Samuel Wickens wrote the first bulldog standard. It was called the Philo Kuon (FEE-lo KAHN) after the author's pen name. A pen name is used instead of an author's own name.

crossbreed —to mate two different breeds of dogs

CHAPTER 3

WRINKLES AND SHORT LEGS

Some people say bulldogs are so ugly, they are cute. The bulldog does indeed look different from most other breeds. Its head is large, its face is short, and its body is thick. These features, along with a mass of wrinkles, give the bulldog its famous sour expression.

Most bulldogs weigh between 40 and 50 pounds (18 and 23 kilograms). They stand 12 to 14 inches (30 to 36 centimeters) tall at the shoulder. A deep chest and broad body gives the dog a sturdy build. Like everything else on the bulldog, its tail is short. It may be straight or spiraled.

A Bulldog's Coat

A bulldog's coat is short, straight, and flat. It may be solid white, red, fawn, or fallow. Fawn is a tan color, and fallow is brown. A bulldog may also be brindle. This is a solid color that is mixed with black or brown hairs. Bulldogs may also be spotted or patched. These types of markings are called piebald.

Bulldogs are
medium-sized dogs.

Eyes and Ears

A bulldog's eyes and ears have a distinct appearance. The breed's ears are rose-shaped. This means the ear folds inward at the bottom and outward at the top. The dog's eyes are set far from its ears and wide apart from each other. They are either black or brown.

A bulldog's short, hanging ears rest close to its head.

A Bulldog's Personality

It is not only the bulldog's look that sets it apart from other breeds. The bulldog has held onto the courage of its ancestors. But modern bulldogs are also known for being calm and loving. If there is one thing a bulldog is not shy about, it is its love for its family. Wherever its owner goes, the bulldog is never far behind.

The combination of a dog's personality and behavior is called its temperament. Most bulldogs have pleasant temperaments. They are very friendly. But they can also be quite stubborn. If your bulldog likes chewing on sneakers, for example, it may take awhile to teach the dog to chew on a dog toy instead.

Being stubborn isn't always a bad thing. This breed's unbending nature can actually help the dogs learn new things. Once a bulldog decides to learn a new trick, nothing can stop it.

At a young age, bulldogs need to learn what is okay for them to chew on.

Bulldogs usually get along well with other pets, but size must be considered when adding a new pet to the household. An excited bulldog can knock over a smaller animal just by being friendly.

Bulldogs adore kids who treat them properly. But like any dog, this breed must also be protected from young children. No animal enjoys having its ears or tail pulled. An adult bulldog could unintentionally hurt a small child due to the dog's size alone.

Bulldogs usually enjoy being around other dogs.

CHAPTER 4

CARING FOR A BULLDOG

Caring for a bulldog is a big responsibility. There are many items owners must buy before bringing a new pet home. There are also several important jobs that must be regularly done for a bulldog.

Bulldog Supplies

Owners should keep their bulldogs safe on walks by using a leash. A bulldog that runs into oncoming traffic is no match for a car. In many places, walking a dog on a leash is required by law. This puts a leash and collar at the top of a new owner's shopping list.

Every bulldog also needs a set of dishes. Stainless steel bowls are the easiest to clean. They can also withstand being knocked over or chewed.

Finally, every bulldog needs toys. The kind your dog likes will depend on its personality. It may enjoy chasing balls or chewing squeaky toys. Try different toys to see what it likes best.

Owners should use a leash when taking their bulldog for a walk.

Bulldog puppies need to eat smaller and more frequent meals than adult bulldogs.

EDGE FACT

Everything your bulldog eats counts. Just a few dog biscuits can contain the same number of calories as a whole bowl of dog food.

Feeding a Bulldog

A bulldog should be fed healthy dog food twice a day. Follow your veterinarian's advice on how much to feed your bulldog. Overfeeding can cause a dog to gain weight. Being overweight increases a dog's risks for many illnesses. It can also lead to hip and knee problems. An owner should also provide a bulldog with fresh drinking water at all times. Empty your dog's dishes and wash them daily. Bacteria grow quickly on dirty dishes.

Exercise

All dogs need regular exercise, but bulldogs require less than most other breeds. Still, they enjoy being outdoors as much as any other dog. Daily walks give a bulldog a chance to stretch its stubby legs. But too much exercise can be hard on this hefty breed's joints.

All dogs enjoy playing outside each day.

The amount of time this breed spends outside can also affect its health. Bulldogs overheat very easily. It is important to keep fresh drinking water out at all times for this reason. Bulldogs, especially white ones, can also get severe sunburns. Planning short periods of outdoor playtime for early morning or late afternoon can help avoid these dangers.

Training a Bulldog

Start training your bulldog the day you bring it home. Puppies often learn new things more quickly than adult dogs. Some people say you can't teach an old dog new tricks. But this saying isn't entirely true. Older dogs can learn new things. It just takes more time and effort from their owners.

Rewarding a bulldog with a treat helps it learn.

Wiping out the wrinkles on a bulldog's face helps keep the dog free of infections.

Bulldogs are very smart. They can be taught to play fetch, follow the leader, and hide and seek. They can even learn to put their own toys away. If you make training fun, your dog will always be interested in learning new things.

Grooming a Bulldog

At first glance, bulldogs do not appear to need much grooming. But just because this breed has short fur doesn't mean it does not need to be kept clean. Regular brushing helps rid a bulldog's coat of dirt and dead hair. Wrinkly bulldogs also need their skin cleaned. Dirt can easily settle into a bulldog's wrinkles. Owners should clean between the folds of skin with a wet cloth or baby wipe every day. The skin then should be dried with a soft cloth.

Keeping a Bulldog Healthy

A yearly trip to the vet helps keep your bulldog healthy. A vet will examine your bulldog by weighing it and listening to its heart. A vet will also check its ears, skin, and joints. Your dog will also receive any **vaccinations** it needs.

Many responsible owners choose to have their bulldogs spayed or neutered at the vet. These surgeries usually take place before the bulldog is one year old. Spaying and neutering prevents certain cancers and helps control the pet population.

Being a responsible owner can help both you and your bulldog get the most out of your time together. Healthy bulldogs can live 10 years or longer. The work you put into caring for this charming breed can be a rewarding experience. The lovable, loyal bulldog will always be at your side.

vaccination — a shot of medicine that protects animals from a disease

Yearly visits to a vet are an important part of caring for a bulldog.

Glossary

breed (BREED) — a certain kind of animal within an animal group; breed also means to mate and raise a certain kind of animal.

breeder (BREE-duhr) — someone who breeds and raises dogs or other animals

breed standard (BREED STAN-derd) — the physical features of a breed that judges look for in a dog show

brindle (BRIN-duhl) — a solid coat color mixed with black or brown hairs

bullbaiting (BUL-bay-ting) — a sport in which a bulldog pulls a bull to the ground by biting its nose

crossbreed (KRAWS-breed) — to mate two different breeds of dogs

piebald (PYE-bawld) — a white coat with patches of other colors

temperament (TEM-pur-uh-muhnt) — the combination of an animal's behavior and personality; the way an animal usually acts or responds to situations shows its temperament.

vaccination (vak-suh-NAY-shun) — a shot of medicine that protects animals from a disease

Read More

Fiedler, Julie. *Bulldogs.* Tough Dogs. New York: PowerKids Press, 2006.

Gray, Susan H. *Bulldogs.* Domestic Dogs. Mankato, Minn.: Child's World, 2008.

Stone, Lynn M. *Bulldogs.* Eye to Eye with Dogs. Vero Beach, Fla.: Rourke, 2007.

Internet Sites

FactHound offers a safe, fun way to find Internet sites related to this book. All of the sites on FactHound have been researched by our staff.

Here's how:

1. Visit *www.facthound.com*
2. Choose your grade level.
3. Type in this book ID **142961952X** for age-appropriate sites. You may also browse subjects by clicking on letters, or by clicking on pictures and words.
4. Click on the **Fetch It** button.

FactHound will fetch the best sites for you!

Index

American Kennel Club
  (AKC), 4, 10
appearance
  coat, 14, 27
  ears, 16, 19, 28
  eyes, 16
  face, 4, 5, 14
  size, 13, 14, 15, 19
  tail, 14, 19
  wrinkles, 14, 26, 27

breeders, 6, 7
breed standard, 10, 13
bullbaiting, 8, 9, 10, 13
bull mastiffs, 12, 13

exercise, 4, 20, 21, 23–24

feeding, 22, 23
French bulldogs, 11, 13

grooming, 26, 27

history, breed, 8, 9, 10, 11, 13

life span, 28

neutering, 28

personality. *See* temperament
puppies, 6, 7, 22, 25

spaying, 28
supplies, 20, 23

temperament, 4, 13, 17–19, 27, 28
training, 25, 27

veterinary care, 28, 29

Wickens, Samuel, 13